DESIRES BECOME DEMONS

FOUR TAMIL POETS

EDITED AND TRANSLATED BY

MEENA KANDASAMY

TILTED AXIS PRESS 2019
THANKS TO OUR KICKSTARTER BACKERS

DESIRES BECOME DEMONS

FOUR TAMIL POETS

EDITED AND TRANSLATED BY
MEENA KANDASAMY

INTRODUCTION

One of the great mythologies of the publishing industry is the purportedly invisible translator. And in a project like this, where the original translator Lakshmi Holmström (1935–2016) has left us, to step in as an editor and a fresh translator involves embodying a ghostly, shadowy persona, lurking in the margins, hiding away behind curtains in the first instance. I hope I shall remain suitably invisible while you allow this work to invigorate you.

Alongside her original translations of the four Tamil poets – Malathi Maithri, Salma, Kutti Revathi and Sukirtharani – first published in 2012 as *Wild Girls, Wicked Words* (a Sangam House-Kalachuvadu Press co-publication), Holmström provided an extensive biographical and bibliographical note on each poet. She painstakingly outlined the background of attacks of their work under the charge of obscenity; she made note of the marginal space given to women writers within the Tamil canon, and she explained the individual stylistic merits of each of the writers in that volume. In order to avoid the reduplication of labour, I will steer clear of that well-trodden ground and instead explore the common threads that hold together this powerful collection.

What draws me to these poets is the manner in which they are political – intensely, unashamedly, unapologetically – and the way in which they see their politics not as something to be pursued outside of or alongside their poetry, but inside it. Their work can be read as a direct engagement with patriarchy, caste and the religiously ordained oppression that has come to represent Tamil culture today. Their poems pose difficult questions in Tamil, and in unmasking a hypocrite society, they prove to be truth-tellers who provide bitter medicine. Each of these poets has an inimitable style: Salma pulls down male privilege and sexual entitlement from its lofty perch in the most beguiling, bedevilled manner; Kutti Revathi achieves such emasculation and dethroning through singular imagery and sheer lyricism; Malathi Maithri taunts and mocks as she deconstructs male fragility in a manner that makes you gleefully applaud; and Sukirtharani fashions a femininity shorn of vulnerability as she delivers death-blows to inequality.

It is essential to resist importing western frameworks – écriture feminine jumps to mind – to read and locate the works of these poets. Yet, it would be a self-defeating omission if one fails to take notice of how their poems make use of man-made, man-splayed, mansplained language. I've included at least a few poems here that explicitly document this wrestle with patriarchal language, challenging male hegemony and inverting the male gaze.

For those familiar with Tamil Sangam poetry – whose antiquity spans from c.300 BCE to 300 CE, and which has left an everlasting imprint on the Tamil imagination – it would not be an exaggeration to say that we had to wait for the emergence of feminist and Dalit poetry to turn certain tropes of universality on their head. On the one hand, the poems included here bitterly rue the valorisation of war which was the mainstay of the heroic *puram* poems; on the other, they question the validity of a collective identity, a universality that is conspicuous by its absence in today's caste-ridden, fragmented society.

As a Tamil woman who was born in the mid-1980s, and who grew up under the larger-than-life backdrop of the Tamil Tigers and their struggle for Eelam liberation, this history is particularly meaningful. Western constructions of feminism see nationalism and feminism as inherently opposed concepts, and likewise, they also tend to deny the agency of women who might join militant movements out of their own free will, consistently portraying them either as victims or gullible recruits. (For academic reading on this subject, refer to the excellent work of Nimmi Gowrinathan.) While the Indian Tamil experience of the Eelam conflict is a protracted second-hand experience of that war, in the work of these poets we find that the articulation and championing of nationalist sentiments in the backdrop of the struggle for self-determination is not mutually exclusive from a simultaneously feminist critique of war, with the inevitable violence and suffering that it entails. It is important to hear the voices of these women poets because we live within the bubble of a so-called progressive Tamil society where even though more than a third of the Tiger fighters were female, women's viewpoints were inevitably written out of the discourse. Perhaps at a later point, it would be interesting to read the work of Tamil women poets from Sri Lanka alongside their Indian and diaspora counterparts; both as a chronicle of war, but also to understand the heart of Tamil resistance to Indian and Hindu imperialism.

I would like to take this opportunity to reflect on the personal connections that I've enjoyed with each of these four firebrand poets. Although I tend to eschew the anecdotal in the everyday in the belief that posturing oneself as anti-gossip is an effective way to refuse to submit to the weight of societal judgment, I make an exception here. All four women poets are a generation older than I am, and although they write in our mother tongue and I write in English, I like to think of how each of us is writing, creating, working from the same milieu – reacting to, and rebelling against, the same casteist, patriarchal elements of our society. Taken together with the Tamil Dalit novelists Bama and Sivakami, I think of women writers as existing in a continuum, our works speaking to each other through time even when we are contemporaries, our interventions into culture carrying the same explosive rage. In 2003, as an eighteen-year-old translator trying to find an illustrator and images for a book of political essays by the Tamil Dalit leader Thirumavalavan, I had the opportunity of meeting Kutti Revathi who had, at that time, just finished making a documentary on my favourite Indian English poet, Kamala Das. My early conversations with her are unforgettable, as is her generous act of introducing me to two artists in Chennai: Benitha Perciyal and Sajitha Shankar, thus opening me to exploring further conversations on women and creativity.

Salma is likewise someone to whom I owe personal gratitude – in the days after I walked out of a bad marriage and met with the radio silence of a judgmental society, she was one of two women from my city who took the time and effort to write to me and ask me how I was doing. It is these individual acts of love and care that forge community, that eventually become support systems. As feminist poets, all of them have not only empowered themselves through their courage of speaking truth to power, but have been comrades-in-arms who have pulled up other women as well. In this context, my greatest debt is to Malathi Maithri. In a publishing landscape rife with caste-based cliques, political fault lines and male privilege, Malathi Maithri and her feminist publishing imprint Ananku proved to be the radical break. Although she did not know me personally, she took the trouble of having my novel translated by her partner Prem, and put me into print in Tamil. Today, our relationship has transformed beyond author-publisher into a friendship that resembles sisterhood. As much as recounting each of these encounters could sound sentimental, I think it is important that we celebrate female love, female bonding, and women empowering each other at every chance we get. It is these stories which provide the perfect foil to patriarchy's favourite myth, the myth of female rivalry.

In putting together this new volume, I have included five poems in Lakshmi Holmström's translation, and I have translated one poem (not included in the earlier volume) from each of the four poets. While Salma and Kutti

Revathi's poems ('Thank You, Marijuana' and 'Tigers', respectively) were solicited for the purpose of this chapbook, my translations of Malathi Maithri and Sukirtharani have a particular history that I would like to share. When hunting for suitable epigraphs to frame each chapter of my novel *When I Hit You*, I was looking for a poem that nailed the vulgar, violative aspects of slut-shaming, and Malathi Maithiri's 'The Thousand and Second Night' put its finger on exactly what I wanted to convey. Its carefully crafted coarseness captures both female humiliation and male insecurity. The choice of 'Pariah God' for Sukirtharani is also deliberate – this was one of several poems of hers that I translated for the essential anthology *No Alphabet in Sight: New Dalit Writing from South India* edited by Susie Tharu and K. Satyanarayana in 2011. As much as it portrays Sukirtharani's characteristic irreverence and anger in the face of caste-ordained language, its tone of defiance also captures the militancy that lies at the heart of the Dalit and anti-caste movement in Tamil Nadu and India today.

To me, the defining aspect of this chapbook is that the poets speak for themselves, prefacing their selected poems briefly, eloquently, and forcefully; the translator-as-interpreter-for-a-western-reader is done away with. They interrogate what the idea of feminism means within a caste-ridden society, and put forth the need to create a feminism based on the inequalities that riddle the Tamil society. Their concerns do not merely end with staking claim to space within the literary world, but they call for a radical upheaval of the unjust structures upon which family and society are both built. The direct address speaks with urgency, and makes one realise that their poems do not live in the golden amber of some historical time, but are, instead, revolutionary interventions in the everyday landscape of Tamil society.

Meena Kandasamy

MALATHI MAITHRI: ON THE MODERN TAMIL LANDSCAPE

So what if we lose our land and our livelihood to imperialist invasions, globalisation, foreign investment — at least we guard the women of our homes from others (read, the oppressed castes)! Such caste-based, Manusmriti-inspired attitudes continue to be the default practice in Indian society from ancient times until today, as evidenced from the routine domestic violence and honour killings of women. This social, familial tradition that treats women as domesticated cattle is being shamelessly heralded by the ruling class as a 'civilised societal more that respects women, worships them as goddesses and is universally praised as pure Hindu religious culture'.

When we emerged on the modern Tamil landscape with our speeches, writings and lifestyles that sought to smash these oppressive structures, we were attacked by the public, our own creative male peers and so-called progressives for being 'immoral, destructive forces' hell-bent on breaking the sacrosanct family unit. History records how imperial rulers sacrificed alternative philosophical traditions that did not adhere to Hinduism or the caste system although they were once cultivated within the ancient Tamil cultural tradition; Tamil empires, who designed their own identities along the lines of the caste-based Brahminical order annihilated Buddhist and Jain literature, its linguistic usages and social discourse which had provided space for women's expression. Only the *Manimekalai* epic managed to escape this systematic devastation and is the solitary extant proto-feminist text.

In the two-thousand-year-old Tamil literary tradition, we can observe that Manusmritibased, casteist and inhumane ideas have been recorded rather vociferously. From Sangam, to Bhakti, to modern literature, the currents of the laws of the patriarchal-Brahmanical Manu continue. In Sangam literature, Avvai stands as the sole voice of feminist politics.

Marxism and feminism emerged to destroy class- and gender-based oppression – but these ideas were philosophically based on the material, social and psychological prototype of white people's lives. Despite its limitations, Marxist philosophy was somewhat accepted by Tamil caste society. This led to the formation of Marxist parties here. Whenever there was talk of Tamil feminism, Tamil Marxist comrades would say: 'That is Western culture, that is not suitable for Indian culture.' This is just one example of why Marxist dialectics did not work. Posturing class struggle as something that implicitly contains the liberation of the oppressed castes and the liberation of women is the worst kind of oppressor-caste, patriarchal domination.

In the context of Dalit political uprising, Tamil feminism was necessitated to function under the identity of Dalit feminism. The casteist Tamil mindset has been irrevocably shaken up by the Dalit political and feminist movement because they have succeeded in delineating, calling out and fighting the various oppressions based on race, language, colour, caste and gender. It must be borne in mind that Tamil Dalit feminist writings against oppression arose from the oppressed women's bodies. When we encounter the words 'women's liberation' we must probe the micro-politics: liberation for women of which caste, which class!

Translated by Meena Kandasamy

TIGER

The tiger sat for a long time
beside the telephone in my house.

When it rose and began to stalk,
the day had darkened.

It blew its warm breath into my ears
as I tried to sleep.
When I turned over, pretending
to be asleep,
before it left us forever
striding past everyone, past everything,
it lay down and rolled over once:
the warmth of my daughter's belly
as she lay beside me
spreading over its face.

When the day dawned, I saw
my daughter; and beside her
a handful of sand
from the island next to ours.

Poems translated by Lakshmi Holmström

SHE WHO THREADS THE SKIES

As the sky fills
the empty shell
after a bird has hatched,
so desire
fills everything.

My daughter threads together
pieces of the sky
scattered by the wing-beat
of migrating birds

like a mysterious game.
The blue sticks to her hands.

SHE WHO ATE THE APPLE

I arrive at an unknown place somewhere.
Slowly I open eyes of hunger
and gaze outward,
clutching the rim of the boat.
And now, suddenly, I see
a shining apple, shedding
a pale red light.
I pluck it and bite deep,
continuing my journey.
After this,
I will never return again
to my own dark lands.

LANGUAGE CHANGE

Endearments become rain
childish prattle becomes birds
gibberish becomes grass
deference becomes a river
tenderness becomes dewfall
humility becomes a moat
requests become curses
entreaty becomes a grave
dreams become cruel gods
abuse becomes chosen gods
desires become demons
silence becomes love
the language of God becomes the night
the language of Satan becomes the day
changing from one to the other
in our dictionary
as if a glass of wine ripples
becoming the wide sea.

INCESSANT WAR

On a summer's day, smouldering intensely
like a forest fire
you returned.

On our seashore, the baby turtles
had shrivelled within their shells.
Even the waves were listless,
losing their serenity.
Dead fish stank, washed ashore.
Not a sound from the crows.

On the stone hearth, the water
was simmering.
You entered my bath-shed
fenced off with palm-leaf matting
and removed your clothes.
I saw bruises all over your body,
your testicles hugely swollen
like the summer's bitter cucumbers.
Shocked, I poured the hot water over you.

Your eyes filled with tears
as you took hold of my hands

which could not fend off
the blows you once rained on me.

The ethnic war continues,
crossing all boundaries.
On that day, though, it raged
like an unquenchable forest fire.

THE THOUSAND AND SECOND NIGHT

Blindfolded, on a blind night
he begins throwing his knives.
Whore, he spits, at she who keeps
thousands of her lovers hidden.
Inside the pillow covers,
the bedspread, the rolled-up mat,
the bookshelf, the attic or the spice-box?
His previous lovers
never caused such betrayal.
Nights thicken into a coir rope
spun out of reproaches.

All his fear:
Will she just knead the dust
to bake a man? That too, with a penis
as large as an elephant's trunk?

The full moon of the thousand and second night
blazes inside his skull.

Translated by Meena Kandasamy

SALMA: ON INTIMACY

Women are people who have been subjected to oppression on the basis of society's idea of femininity. Women are creatures who occupy the suffocating space fashioned through centuries of identities and ideologies. Feminism is women becoming self-aware and liberating themselves from the state of losing their individuality as a result of being conditioned to believe in regressive ideas. Feminism is leading an independent life in an equal space. Feminism is a rejection of the institutions of caste and religion which were created to subjugate women, it is the seeking of a space for herself where she attains freedom from a sad life intertwined with the conspiracy of these structures. I think feminism is a departure from the false hierarchies of man and woman. Feminism is women returning to a life that existed before difference and discrimination reared their heads.

The injustice against a woman begins on the basis of her gender, following which she is subjected to violence and suffering – I feel that the form and genre of poetry aid me, or rather, give me the freedom to capture this in an emotionally charged manner. In my poems I have focussed on the difficulties faced by other women too, moving beyond my personal life and the struggles that I have faced. When the voice that has been held, stagnated, is instead expressed blatantly, emphasizing its vigour, vibrancy and anger, it automatically centralises feminist politics within the poem.

A feminist reading begins in the perspective of the reader. The questions that I raise within my creative work, the criticisms that I place through them, the beliefs that I seek to demolish – these are for the readers to digest. It is possible that it makes a few people think, that it hurts a few others, that it makes a few people disagree. But under some particular circumstance, when the readers proceed towards establishing an intimacy with the writing, I think they will be able to understand the meaning of feminism.

Translated by Meena Kandasamy

A MIDNIGHT TALE

These nights
following the children's birth
you seek, dissatisfied,
within the nakedness you know so well,
my once unblemished beauty.

You are much repelled,
you say,
by a thickened body
and a belly criss-crossed with birthmarks;
my body, though, is unchanging
you say
today, hereafter and for evermore.

My voice, deep-buried
in the valley of silence,
mutters to itself:

True indeed,
your body is not like mine:
it proclaims itself,
it stands manifest.

Before this too,
your children, perhaps, were born
in many places, to many others;
you may be proud
you bear no traces of their birth.

And what must I do?
These birthmarks cannot be
repaired, any more than my own decline –
this body isn't paper
to cut and paste together, or restore.

Nature has been
more perfidious to me
than even you;
but from you began
the first stage of my downfall.

More bizarre
than the early hours of night
is the hour past midnight
when dreams teem.

It is now, at this midnight hour
the tiger which sat quietly

within the picture on the wall
takes its place at my head
and stares
and stares.

Poems translated by Lakshmi Holmström

THE CONTRACT

Always
my sister will repeat in anger
what Amma says more subtly:
that I am to blame
for all that goes wrong
in the bedroom.

Every day, in the bedroom
these are the first words to greet me:
'So what is it, today?'
Often
they are
the last words, too.

From a thousand shimmering stars
pointing fingers accuse me of whoredom
– once again –
and counsels float into the trembling night.

The childlike sobbing of a cat
unable to feed its litter
seizes me by the entrails.

You too
may have your complaints
but Time and our history
make very clear
where I now stand:

To receive a little love
– however tarnished –
from you

To fulfil my responsibility
as your child's mother

To buy from the outside world
my sanitary napkins and contraceptives
and for many other little favours

To hold a little authority over you
if possible

To strengthen what authority I have
Just a little

In full knowledge of all this
my vagina opens.

THE WORM

The worm appears, slithering in the food
as, with extreme hunger,
I prepare to eat.

There is no reason for me to be hostile
towards this slithering and sliding
green, soft body.

Even though I learn to cast it aside
and continue to eat, every day
it appears quietly, creeping towards me.

Today, I begin to learn
to endure it.

In the years to come
it grows, shifts shape
climbs on me and crawls about
sucking its food from my body

frightening me
with its stranglehold
of possibilities.

AT THE MOMENT OF PARTING

Before I parted from you
I had hoped to see
whether

the evening which falls upon
my front courtyard, scattering
seeds of desire
falls upon you and your house too
in exactly the same way.

CHARIOT OF DARKNESS

The children's daybreak always waits
until I have opened my eyes.
Every day, with their petitions,
they draw out my dawn
from the night's heavy darkness.
The elder boy, tearful eyes sparkling,
claiming his prerogative for the first bath,
waits for my consent, while the younger one
who swallowed the last drop of my breast milk
clamours loudly, voicing the privilege
of the very young. The very house shudders.

A monstrous picture of my neglect
lies stagnant, immoveable, always
in my eldest son's heart.
It disturbs the impartiality of my love;
tilts it momentarily.

They churn my motherhood
with their tears,
and measure out their share
of the massing love.
Though their tender hearts

plant seeds of weariness alone,
yet
with my sons' help
I will take hold of the rope
and haul away the darkness
always by my side
like an unmoving chariot.

THANK YOU, MARIJUANA

I did not know if it was me,
that this was who I was
until I smoked ganja
inhaling it all the way.

Even I had not known
that my body, created from
a rib taken from the man's, could
sprout wings, that my body
was a hawk under the tartness
of a wine that went into me
with the sharpness of swords,
that the burning darkness
of midnight hours could be
torn apart by total nudity.

Not like what someone said –
that I would unburden the demons
hiding inside my head after a few kisses.

This body of mine is made
of the dirt of earth, and is intense
like withering, wandering clouds.

Tonight, for the first time,
I am bringing along,
my body that I did not know.
Thank you, marijuana
for letting us meet.

Translated by Meena Kandasamy

KUTTI REVATHI: ON THE QUESTION OF ORGANISING AND MOBILISING

The definition and function of feminism changes from country to country. For the kind of feminist action required in India to exist, it is essential to understand the caste system. Otherwise, we cannot create a feminism that is strong enough to resist it. Those who spoke feminism in the last century were all caste-Hindus, and of dominant caste. The feminism they articulated secured their rights through their caste. Although it appeared on the surface level that these women had been empowered, it was merely their specific caste structures, Hindutva and Brahminism, that were empowered. Women were reduced to bringing power to an enslaving structure. Therefore, if we do not understand the caste system, we cannot create a truly emancipatory feminism.

Every year, violent acts against women and children continue to increase in number and intensity. Even today, we have not been able to create a 'pressure group' that can reform our state or our society. Research suggests that post-1975 there was no conducive scenario for women to organise and mobilise themselves. Caste remains a barrier preventing women from coming together.

The dominant-caste male, the dominant-caste female, the Dalit male, the Dalit female – such are the gradations of the caste ladder. When men of the oppressed castes are kept a rung below the women of the dominant castes, feminism has to take this into consideration in its own evolution. Women poets and artists who wrote in the last century from the perspective of women's liberation were putting forth ideas of sexuality, desire and individuality – but these ideas only addressed their personal liberation. Certainly, these ideas did not benefit other women associated with them in any manner. Today, I feel a sense of contradiction even reading the likes of women poets such as Kamala Das.

Even after so much violence and sacrifice, even after we have lost our own sisters and children to caste hatred, we have not understood its problematic nature. We must first realise the shortcomings of not having a united feminist movement that can command the state strongly on the rights of women and emphasise its importance to society at large.

In truth, what goes by the name of feminism here is the adoption and introduction of women's rights as they exist abroad, particularly America and Europe. Our feminist thoughts have been strengthened along the lines of Phule, Ambedkar, Periyar – and even these male intellectuals became feminists because they realised that caste differences kept women apart and separated them. If these leaders did not exist, we would be bereft of the social philosophy which allows us to understand the problems of women today – and India would have been a dismal continent.

But in this social setup, when women mobilise together for an issue, the movement is destroyed because dominant-caste women wage power struggles. Caste is a system of hierarchy that prevents women from coming together even under the umbrella of women's rights. Even though a woman may have a high social profile, if she happens to be a Dalit, or low in terms of her caste identity, other dominant-caste women will behave in such a manner as to prevent this woman from attaining a leadership position within the movement. The 'reason' they put forward is that women of their castes would not join a movement where Dalit or oppressed-caste women are in the majority or where they are in charge of the leadership.

For these dominant-caste women, there exist no problems in functioning alongside powerful men. At the same time, in the public sphere they will mouth general arguments against male domination and portray men as enemies. Oppressor-caste women will even wear the mask of academic and institutionalised feminism to go about doing this. Such feminists have a very selfish motive, they want to flaunt and entrench their identity in the public sphere in a formidable manner. When it comes to the larger question of women's rights and problems, they lose their sense of solidarity by waging petty power struggles – such as the fights between a mother-in-law and daughter-in-law.

Translated by Meena Kandasamy

LIGHT IS A PROWLING CAT

Opening the door noiselessly,
Light puts out a hand
– hesitantly –
wondering if it's still raining.

Seeing that the rain has gone
it spreads out its shadow-shop
upon the clustering trees,
then climbs up the tent-face
to sit and watch the world.

Scattered upon the earth, the beauty of cat-colours.

When its shadow starts to eat itself
Light slithers down the tree and springs
right up to the lamp in its niche.

Now Light perches on Night's back
which stands erect as a compound wall
and takes for its own

the great shining light of lovers' union
through the moon's wide eyes.

Poems translated by Lakshmi Holmström

BREASTS

Breasts
are bubbles, rising from marshlands.

As they gently swelled and blossomed
at due season, at Time's edge,
I watched over them in amazement.

Never speaking to anyone else
they are with me always
singing
of quiet sorrow
of love
of ecstasy.

They have never forgotten
to enthuse the seedbeds
of all my changing seasons.

At times of penance
they struggle and strain;
and at the thrust and pull of lust
like the proud ascent of music
they stand erect.

From the press of an embrace
they distil love; from the shock
of childbirth
milk, flowing from blood.

Like two teardrops,
which cannot be wiped away
when love is thwarted,
they fill, and they overflow.

THE SEA-FETTERED ISLAND

Those who believed that the waves
lapping at their feet were themselves the sea
stayed safe, within their peninsula.

There, where the waves hide the island
tears are salt,
poetry is salt, sex is salt,
the sun's burning finger is salt, love is salt,
the roots of medicinal herbs are salt,
bodily pain is salt.
There, tears are indeed salt.

Even at this distance
a sourness belches from the heart
like an enemy;
a fear is felt, as when a friend is ill.
Yet no one will hold their breath
and cross the sea to the island.

The island is a raft,
the raft a pot of fire,
Sri Lanka, burning.

STONE GODDESSES

The sculpture, peeling away its skin
of stone, and coming to life,
too shy of the light,
becomes a dark shape
lurking within its curtain of shadows.

Time's nail
hammered to its feet
has cursed the rain and the wind

also
the flung droppings of bats
and the desolate spaces of solitude.

It is possible that
sculptures overflowing with God's grace
walk about as goddesses
where man's gaze is unknown,
in ruined halls, perhaps,
or in the recesses of tall temple towers

But, for some reason,
at the merest hint of man's scent
they decline into lifeless corpses.

FLOODGATES OF MEMORY

The floodgates of your memory
overflow across my heat-ridden land
heralding the monsoon.
With unending ardour and foaming insolence
memory covers my earth with potholes.
It crumples and throws away early mornings
full of boredom, as though the same day
were to be endured a thousand times over.
Like light it tunnels its way into the cave.
I'm aware of its hissing anger but
I scoop it up with scorched hands and drink.
My gaze wanders through tall trees,
alighting with joy
on a wondrous kurinchi flower.

Let not our parting
blast through the horizon.
May the force of our love
leap like a bird whose wings
will never be caught in a net.
Every spilt drop of it may one day
touch the very womb of the sea.

The flood of your memory
opens the sluice gate of my vagina.

TIGERS

I am the tiger, and you, the tigress.
We show each other the depths
of our strength – biting with mouths
meant to give love, leaving marks
on our bodies with sharp claws.

Tender leaf shoots inlaid in your eyes
will hide you in the forest, I will play hide
and seek between the trees, and,
in the nights as we make love
the desire for you that I kept hidden
away until then will proclaim itself aloud.

Fragrant as thalampoo,
the hiding places within my organs
are meant for you. As our cubs suck
on milk from your mammaries
spurting like mountain springs,
I will be lying there, ignoring your love.

When you could not hunt me
I would stroke your hair.
When you suffocate, unable

to digest my presence, you'll
tremble to become my prey
And I'll hunt you down.

This is how, in later days,
I became the tigress
and you became the tiger.

Translated by Meena Kandasamy

SUKIRATHARANI: ON BODIES AND AUTONOMY

The first oppression in the history of the world is the oppression of women. What was a matrilineal society has, over the course of time, ended up as a patriarchal society. Caste, religion and family – everything functions as structures to oppress women. A society that ingrains caste and untouchability attains the form of a magnified family. The structure of family which ingrains the subjugation of women and the concepts of ritual pollution functions as a miniature version of society. Without the destruction of these structures, it is not possible to achieve women's liberation.

Just as caste annihilation becomes possible

when equality, fraternity and liberty are strengthened, likewise, women's liberation becomes a possibility only when gender equality becomes rooted within the family. Women's liberation and women's freedom are at the core of feminism, to which we cannot ascribe a blanket definition. This is because feminism can vary according to language, place, time, circumstance and culture. Feminism can thus change from one milieu to the next.

To me, feminism is the agitational efforts of men and women against the patriarchal oppression of women, against the oppressive systems of caste, religion, family and power. Feminism is not against men, it is against male power. Women's freedom is the right to do what a woman wants to do, and the right to not do what she does not want to do. In short, when one has internal and external autonomy – that is women's liberation, and the movement towards this is feminism.

It becomes essential in my work to question and counter and oppose all forms of power and oppression that are foisted on women mentally, physically and without their consent. Also, one has to destroy societal judgments and traditional norms which are placed on women. One has to question the manner in which the values of love, desire, courage are seen and presented as masculine and belonging to men, and simultaneously how women are subjugated through their portrayal as the proponents of mercy.

Women's bodies are not meant for men; a woman's body is meant for herself. I want to prove all this through my poetry, and this is what I continue to do.

Translated by Meena Kandasamy

INFANT LANGUAGE

I need a language
still afloat in the womb
which no one has spoken so far,
which is not conveyed through signs and gestures.
It will be open and honourable,
not hiding in my torn underclothes.
It will contain a thousand words
which won't stab you in the back
as you pass by.
The late night dreams I memorised –
hoping to share them –
will not be taken for complaints.
Its meanings will be as wide as the skies.
Its gentle words won't wound
the tender surface of the tongue.
The keys of that unique language
will put an end to sorrow,
make way for a special pride.

You will read there my alphabet, and feel afraid.

You will plead with me in words
that are bitter, sour and putrid
to go back to my shards of darkened glass.

And I shall write about that too, bluntly,
in an infant language, sticky with blood.

Poems translated by Lakshmi Holmström

I SPEAK UP BLUNTLY

I shooed away crows
while flaying dead cows of their skin.
Stood for hours, waiting
to eat the town's leavings –
then boasted that I ate hot, freshly cooked rice.
When I saw my father in the street
the leather drum slung from his neck,
I turned my face away
and passed him by.
Because I wouldn't reveal
my father's job, his income,
the teacher hit me.
Friendless, I sat alone
on the back bench, weeping,
though no one knew.

But now
if anyone asks me
I speak up bluntly:
I am a Paraichi.

A FAINT SMELL OF MEAT

In their minds
I, who smell faintly of meat,
my house where bones hang
stripped entirely of flesh,
and my street
where young men wander without restraint
making loud music
from coconut shells strung with skin
are all at the furthest point of our town.
But I, I keep assuring them
we stand at the forefront.

EVERY TOWN IS A HOMETOWN, ALL PEOPLE ARE KIN*

All people can be inspectors:
those who betrayed,
those who murdered,
those who incited to murder,
idle spectators,
those whose blood boiled in their veins,
those who were silent witnesses.

All places can be inspected:
canals caked with blood,
torture chambers devoid of humanity,
pitiless refugee camps.

All things may be renovated:
ruined buildings,
burnt-down hutments,
bullet-pierced windows.

At all times, homage may be paid:
after life has gone,
after the grass has grown over

burial mounds.

Any language may be spoken:
the English of the gazettes,
the Hindi of the rulers,
Chinese, dripping poison,
Sinhala, drunk with hatred,
high Tamil, stripped naked.

A carpet may be spread for anyone:
spread for the Buddha bathed in blood,
and also for the weaver
of the same blood-stained carpet.

Anyone may do anything
for every town is a hometown,
all people are kin.

---

* *The title repeats, with great irony, one of the best-known lines from* Purananuru *(c. 2nd century AD): 'Yaadum ure, yaavarum kelir.'*

THE ONLY WOMAN
IN THE WORLD

Her skin glints
like unmined gold ore.
Her leafy eyebrows have not been tamed
nor has she bathed
in some luxurious milk.
Her eyes wander, dispassionately.
She wears about her waist
the dried skin of a polar bear,
she carries in her hands
sharp weapons of flint.
Her feast is laid out on olive branches:
roasted meat, roots, fruit.
She rises and walks away
to break down branches of trees
where no bird has built its nest:
the only woman in the world,
the first woman, bearing
no scar of an umbilical cord.
Innumerable men turned to stone,
wait, aeon upon aeon,

to be released from their curse
by the touch of her feet.

PARIAH GOD

You say
the heat that sears your side
is a pariah sun.

You say
the beak that steals
the worm-ridden grain spread out to sun
is a pariah crow.

You say
the mouth that snatches
food along with your wrist
is a pariah dog.

When the land is tilled
and sweat is sown,
you say
it is pariah labour.

If this is how everything is named,
what is the name of that pariah god
who walks the earth blood-thirsty?

Translated by Meena Kandasamy

Copyright
© Malathi Maithri, Salma, Kutti Revathi, and Sukirtharani 2019
Translations copyright © Lakshmi Holmström and Meena Kandasamy 2019

This edition published in the United Kingdom by Tilted Axis Press in 2019. This translation was funded by Arts Council England and 278 brilliant Kickstarter backers. Thank you!

The poems in Lakshmi Holmström's translations first appeared in *Wild Girls, Wicked Words*, a 2012 Sangam House-Kalachuvadu Press co-publication.

tiltedaxispress.com

The rights of the authors of these works to be identified as such, and those of Lakshmi Holmström and Meena Kandasamy as the translators, have been asserted in accordance with Section 77 of the Copyright, Designs and Patent Act 1988.

This is a work of fiction. Names, characters, places and incidents are either the product of the author's imagination or are used fictitiously. Any resemblance to any actual persons, living or dead, events or locales is entirely coincidental.

ISBN (chapbook)   9781911284260
ISBN (ebook)   9781911284338

A catalogue record for this book is available from the British Library.

Edited by Saba Ahmed
Cover design by Soraya Gilanni Viljoen
Typesetting and ebook production by Simon Collinson
Printed and bound by Footprint Workers Co-op, Leeds

Yeoyu— new voices Korea

Eight exquisitely designed & highly collectible chapbooks with enthralling new short stories from:

Han Kang	tr. Deborah Smith
Cheon Heerahn	tr. Emily Yae Won
Han Yujoo	tr. Janet Min
Bae Suah	tr. Deborah Smith
Jeon Sung-tae	tr. Sora Kim-Russell
Hwang Jeung-eun	tr. Jeon Seung-hee
Kang Hwa Gil	tr. Mattho Mandersloot
Kim Soom	tr. Emily Yae Won

www.strangers.press/yeoyu £35